W9-BOU-793

Rookie Read-About® Science

When You Look Up at the Moon

By Allan Fowler

Consultants:
Robert L. Hillerich, Professor Emeritus,
Bowling Green State University, Bowling Green, Ohio
Consultant, Pinellas County Schools, Florida

Lynne Kepler, Educational Consultant

Fay Robinson, Child Development Specialist

CHILDRENS PRESS ®
CHICAGO

Design by Lindaanne Donohoe

Library of Congress Cataloging-in-Publication Data

Fowler, Allan.
    When you look up at the moon/by Allan Fowler.
       p. cm. — (Rookie read-about science)
    ISBN 0-516-06025-2
    1. Moon — Exploration — Juvenile literature. [1. Moon —
Exploration.]   I. Title. II. Series: Fowler, Allan. Rookie read-about science.

QB582.F69 1994
523.3 — dc20

93-38589
CIP
AC

20744

When you look up at the moon, do you wish you could visit it?

Here's what you'd see there —

very tall mountains,

wide flat plains, and

big rings called craters.

Rocks would be all around you.

But not a single tree
or blade of grass.

Since the moon has
no air or water,
plants and animals can't
live there.

Has anybody ever visited the moon?

Yes — twelve astronauts.

Six American spaceships made trips to the moon.

The first trip was in 1969;

the last was in 1972.

And each time,
two astronauts
stepped
onto the moon's
surface.

They wore spacesuits that

gave them air to breathe.

They could jump
higher on the moon
than they could on
Earth, and
they came down
more slowly.

It was almost like
floating!

From the moon,
the astronauts
could see Earth.

This is how it looked
to them.

About every four weeks,
the moon travels in a
complete circle around
Earth.

The sun shines
on the moon and
lights it up.

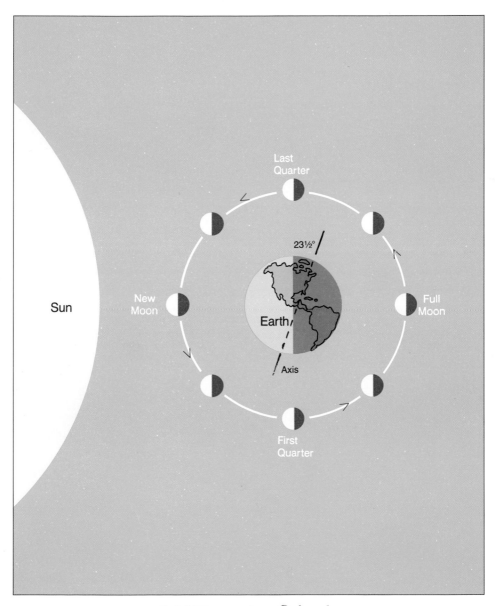

23

That's why you
can see it.

When you see it
as a bright circle,
it's called a
full moon.

Some nights the moon

looks more like this . . .

or like this half-moon . . .

or like this crescent moon.

Now that you know more about the moon, would you still like to visit it?

Maybe someday you can.

Words You Know

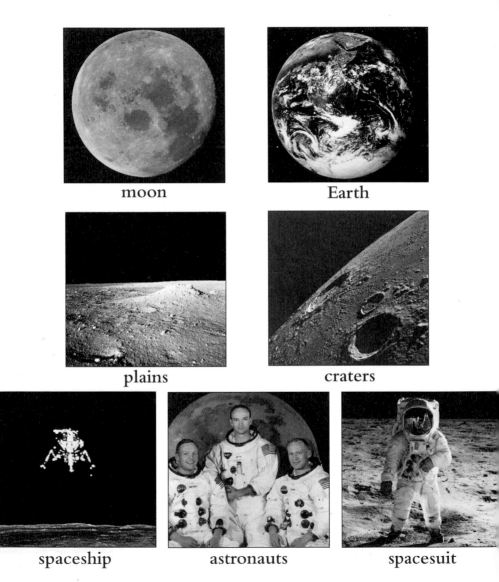

moon

Earth

plains

craters

spaceship

astronauts

spacesuit

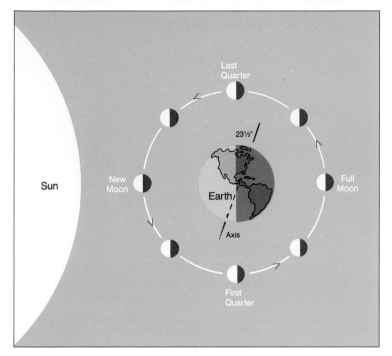

The moon travels around the Earth.

full moon   half-moon   crescent moon

31

Index

About the Author

Allan Fowler is a free-lance writer with a background in advertising. Born in New York, he lives in Chicago now and enjoys traveling.

Photo Credits

NASA – 6, 9, 13, 15, 16, 21, 30 (top left, center right, bottom right)

PhotoEdit – Air & Space Museum, Washington, D.C., ©Paul Conklin, 17; ©Myrleen Ferguson Cate, 29

Photri – 4, 5, 7, 10, 12, 19, 30 (center left, bottom center)

Tom Stack & Associates – ©Dave Fleetham, 3

SuperStock International, Inc. – 11, 30 (bottom left); ©NASA (top right)

Valan – ©Dr. A. Farquhar, cover, 25, 31 (bottom left); ©J. Eastcott/Y. Momatiuk, 26; ©Pierre R. Chabot, 27, 31(bottom center); ©J.R. Page, 28, 31 (bottom right)

Art by Chuck Hills – 23, 31 (top)

COVER: Moon over lake